BEAUTIFUL

Sydney

BEAUTIFUL

Sydney

*S*tanding sentinel at the entrance to the historic Sydney Cove,
site of Australia's first permanent white settlement over
200 years ago, is the Sydney Opera House. Since its completion
in 1973, the Opera House has become one of the city's best-known
and most often used landmarks. It also forms the nucleus of
Sydney's performing arts, with its main auditorium seating
2,690 people. Viewed here from the Opera House forecourt, it
is dramatically lit after dark, providing a spectacular venue for
opera, ballet, drama and orchestral music.

Left: *Sydney is a modern commercial city with a dramatic profile. A stone's throw from the commercial towers of the central business district, the Opera House is Sydney's cultural centre, and a focal point of the city.*
Above: *Centrepoint Tower is 305 metres high, and features prominently on the skyline, seen here at dusk.*
Below: *The Sydney Harbour Bridge, a feat of modern engineering which revolutionised the city's communication and transport systems, was opened in 1932 to link the city centre and its southern suburbs with the northern sector of the city and the country beyond. The magnificent steel arch of the Bridge rises the equivalent of 40 storeys above the water.*

Opposite, top: *Some of downtown Sydney's great high-rise buildings, dominated by Centrepoint Tower.*

Opposite, bottom: *Sydney maintains strong links with its past, as with this replica of H.M.S. Bounty of Captain Bligh fame.*

Below: *Viewed from Darling Harbour, Sydney's newest entertainment, convention and exhibition centre, the central business district takes on quite a different look.*

Right: *The Opera House's glittering, sail-like roofs are no accident. The 'sails', a reminder of the sailing ships that played such an important part in the city's past, are covered by hundreds of thousands of white tiles, reflecting the sunlight and giving the structure its strong, clean lines.*

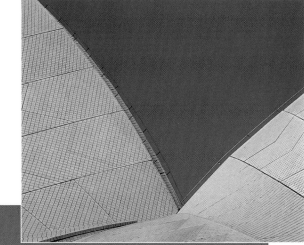

Above: *Warm, still, bright summer days are typical of Sydney and are often followed by a cooling southerly breeze or by short but spectacular electrical storms. Here, the evening lights of the floating city vie in brightness with nature's spectacular lightning display over Sydney Cove. The Cove is the city terminal for the Sydney Harbour ferries, which provide an extensive passage service to many harbourside suburbs. These ferries are a feature of the city, and many citizens regard them with great affection for the tranquil mode of travel they offer between quiet suburban wharves and the bustle of Australia's greatest commercial centre.*

Above: *Woolloomooloo Valley and Bay, the Botanic Gardens and the business district beyond, seen from Kings Cross.* Opposite, top: *Closer to the ground, Kings Cross is a part of the city that never sleeps. Dedicated to the entertainment of the city's visitors and its young residents, this is a busy after-dark area, packed with nightclubs, restaurants, strip clubs and tourist shops.*

Opposite, bottom: *Martin Place, which was closed to traffic in the 1970s, is now a wide pedestrian mall with a fountain, amphitheatre and sculptures, and serves as the central business district's city square. It is flanked by some of the city's most prestigious high-rise buildings, and is a pleasant, leafy enclave amid the heavily developed banking and commercial precinct.*

Opposite, top: *The centre of Sydney and the Darling Harbour Development are linked by a monorail, the latest addition to the city's transport systems. The city is also served by an extensive underground and surface electrical rail system, a network of harbour ferries and a large fleet of efficient buses.*

Left: *While the eastern part of the harbour is used primarily for recreation purposes, to the west of the Sydney Harbour Bridge lies the working harbour which is devoted principally to cargo handling, shipbuilding and repairs.*

Below: *The Opera House, with Sydney Cove and the Botanic Gardens behind. The Opera House comprises much more than the obvious shells, which cover only part of the waterfront area with its wide walkways and restaurants.*

Above: *The annual Ferrython is one of the highlights of the Australia Day celebrations on Sydney Harbour. Ferries are decorated with ribbons and balloons and, starting just below Harbour Bridge, race upstream and back, accompanied by flotillas of pleasure craft.*

Left: *Nearly 30,000 runners stream through Sydney's streets in the City to Surf Fun Run each August.*

Opposite, top: *Sydney Harbour from North Head – spectacular on a sunny day, tranquil and impressive at sunset.*

Opposite, bottom: *The Botanic Gardens, situated between the city centre and the harbour, was the site of the city's first farm. As well as being one of the world's great botanic display and research centres, it is now also the site of many memorials. This one honours Captain Arthur Phillip, the first colonial governor of New South Wales.*

Above: *This pavement café is part of the Darling Harbour Development, a project which turned commercial wharves and a railyard into a popular waterside attraction, to mark the city's Bicentennial in 1988.*
Right: *Darling Harbour, the central business district's western water flank, also features the National Maritime Museum, aquarium and Chinese Gardens.*
Below: *The light, modern architecture and pedestrian malls of this centre are characteristic of much of Sydney's recent development.*

Opposite, top: *Sydney is at once Australia's most important business, financial, trading and industrial centre and a shopping Mecca for citizens and visitors alike. The Sydney shopping experience covers a range of possibilities, from large department stores to informal traders, like this well-stocked flower seller.*

Left: *Rowers slice through the water in front of the Darling Harbour Development and the Novotel Hotel.*

Above: *A landmark of old Sydney, the Lord Nelson Hotel is situated in the historic Rocks district. It is thought to be the oldest surviving hotel in Sydney, and is typical of the many historic buildings in this charming part of the city.*

Below: *Darling Harbour is the site of the National Maritime Museum, completed in 1992. It has an extensive and varied collection of maritime exhibits and artefacts relating to Australia's history, including the ships and boats moored alongside the building.*

Left: *Sydney's centre is a shopper's paradise, not only for the quality and variety of goods available but also for the pleasure of finding treasures in the city's beautiful arcades and shopping centres. An example of such a shopping arcade is the Queen Victoria Building, an old commercial structure which has been refurbished for easy strolling and casual browsing among the many small shops.*

Below: *Sydney Harbour's western basin – suburbs and docklands form this part of the Harbour, which is less frequented by tourists than the area east of Harbour Bridge.*

Opposite, top: *Sydney is not all hustle and bustle, and there are many peaceful spots. Government House, the official residence of the New South Wales State Governor, is set in the tranquil Botanic Gardens.*

Opposite, bottom: *Alongside ultra-modern commercial towers, many of Sydney's older generation Art-Deco buildings remain, such as the Grace Building in King Street. In the background is Centrepoint Tower.*

Opposite, top: *Sydney is home to a large ethnic Chinese population and has a busy and extensive Chinatown. Nearby, as part of the Darling Harbour Development, is a reconstruction of a traditional Chinese garden.*

Opposite, bottom: *Each year in March, Sydney is host to the Annual Gay and Lesbian Mardi Gras Parade, which winds down the length of Oxford Street from the city to the eastern suburbs.*
Above: *All along the shores of Sydney Harbour, the suburbs seem to tumble down toward the water from the surrounding high ridges. Balmain is one of them – a popular and fashionable restored suburb to the west of the Harbour Bridge.*
Right: *Busking and street theatre are popular activities in Sydney, and nowhere are they more in evidence than at Sydney Cove. Here a one-man band performs against the background of a ferry.*

Left: *The commercial area
has spread widely into the city's older,
surrounding residential areas, such as
East Sydney, where new, tall buildings
mix with the older, lower structures.*
Opposite, bottom: *Sydney's surviving
Art-Deco buildings, with their ornate
bas-relief sculptures, provide visual
variety. The City Mutual Building
on Hunter Street was built in 1936.*
Above: *The Rocks is an old, inner-city
district, which has been preserved and
restored as a reminder of early Sydney.
The busy covered market shown here,
which has over 120 stalls, and many small
specialty shops make it an interesting area
for browsing, as well as a popular destina-
tion for tourists.*
Right: *A study in contrasts – the historic
Rocks district is seen here against a back-
drop of high-rise commercial buildings,
highlighting the city's varied and
colourful history.*

Left and opposite, top: *Taronga Park Zoo is one of the city's most popular attractions, both for its spectacular setting and for its outstanding collections of native and exotic animals, such as these giraffes and orang-utans. The zoo has a continuing programme of reconstruction, aimed at providing the animals with a safe haven which closely approximates their native environment.*

Below: *Hyde Park is the central business district's principal green lung, a place of quiet walks, shady trees and tailored lawns. One of its landmarks is the Archibald Fountain (opposite, bottom), donated to the city by one of its great benefactors. Its spray provides a welcome coolness to the park's strollers.*

Above: *For much of Sydney and many Sydneysiders, winter is simply an inconvenient interlude between swimming seasons. Colourful beach clothing adorns the young and tanned, advertising the delights of distant resorts! If the weather is good, and it usually is, the city's ocean beaches attract surfers and sunbathers in large numbers, as here at Bondi Beach* (right).

Opposite, bottom: *Sydney's life-savers, as well as mounting beach patrols and engaging in surf rescues, use surfboats for mass or distant rescues. Although they now use fast, outboard-powered inflatables, they maintain their skills on the older rowed surfboats.*

Left: *Bondi Beach is the most famous of the 52 ocean beaches on Sydney's Pacific fringe, providing colourful and constantly changing vistas.*
Opposite, bottom: *The Surf Life-saving Association keeps its members in top physical condition.*
Top: *North of the Harbour, the great beaches continue. Manly, easily accessible from the city centre by ferry and fast catamaran, is one of the most popular and patronised stretches of the Northern Beaches. As with Sydney's other beaches, Manly is patrolled and protected by volunteer life-savers* (above).

Above: Sydney is bounded on the north side by the Hawkesbury River, which flows into the Pacific Ocean through Broken Bay. The river and the bay are both very popular boating waters. Moored at tranquil Bobbin Head on the lower reaches of the Hawkesbury are some of Sydney's 250,000 pleasure boats.

Below: If you are not swimming or sunbathing during a Sydney summer, you will in all likelihood be sailing. Even in the confined waters of the city centre's Darling Harbour, sailing boats abound.

Right: Sydney Cricket Ground was the birthplace of international one-day cricket as well as day-night games, a combination that always draws enthusiastic crowds.

Left and opposite, below: *Sydney's most northerly suburb is the exclusive Palm Beach, originally a weekend retreat for the city's wealthiest residents. Featuring a beautiful beach, it consists of a narrow strip of land bounded on one side by the Pacific Ocean and on the other by the sheltered waters of Broken Bay, a popular spot for the city's multitude of pleasure sailors.* Below: *The Sydney Basin is surrounded by rugged sandstone ramparts, which edge the drowned river valley of the great Hawkesbury River. On this river lies Bobbin Head, a boating venue close to Sydney's northern suburbs.*

Left: *At the western edge of the Sydney Basin lie the Blue Mountains, a spur of the Great Dividing Range which runs down the east side of the continent. This is a land of deeply fractured and wildly rugged sandstone hills, of steep cliffs, of valleys and ridges covered thickly with trees. The Three Sisters, shown here, form a distinctive feature at Katoomba. Lined with steep mountain rivers and streams, the Blue Mountains lie in a high-rainfall area and are snow-capped in winter. Cascades such as the Empress Falls (opposite, bottom) plunge through tangled vegetation, bringing coolness during the warm summers and attracting wildlife to the region.* Above: *Sheer cliffs long defeated early efforts by the first settlers to cross over the mountains from Sydney to the fertile plains beyond. Today the same cliffs provide worthy challenges for rock climbers.*

Left: *A huge part of the Blue Mountains region has been declared a national park, of which there are several within easy reach of Sydney. This ensures the continued protection of such sights as Bridal Veil Falls and Hanging Swamp at Govett's Leap, featured here.*
Right: *The Sydney Plain, the Hawkesbury River Valley and the Blue Mountains are home to a great number of birds, many of them brightly adorned with spectacular colours. Shown here is the rainbow lorikeet, a common sight in this area.*
Below: *The environs of Sydney are rich in native animals. Among the more prevalent of these, even in suburban Sydney, is the common brushtail possum, a mainly nocturnal creature.*

Left: *While Australia is often described as a dry continent, its east coast and hinterland enjoy excellent rains. Many rivers rise along the Divide and provide water for the fertile valleys and plains all along this coast. The Paddy's River Falls on the Southwest Slopes are a dramatic sight.*

Top: *The magnificent Blue Mountains, where summers are mild and winters sharp with occasional snows, attract both Sydney residents and visitors. Their rocky grandeur, easy walks and beautiful waters, so close to Sydney, should not be missed.*

Above: *Although kangaroos can be seen in special reserves and fauna parks, one does not have to travel far from the city to see Australia's national symbol in the wild.*

Opposite, top: *For sportsmen and sportswomen of all kinds, Sydney and the area surrounding the city offer virtually unlimited opportunities to pursue their outdoor interests. The Wollondilly River on the outskirts of Sydney, for instance, attracts fly-fishermen.*

Left: *On the western edge of the Blue Mountains lies the fertile Hartley Vale. The Vale, a well-established and highly productive region, lies between the Blue Mountains and the Great Divide.*

Above: *The New South Wales coastal plain, which stretches the whole length of the state's coast, provides endless vistas of great beauty. Dawn sheds its golden light near Bega on the South Coast.*

Right: *The golden wattle, Australia's official floral symbol, forms a colourful display right across Sydney every spring.*

Above: *Quiet, beautiful and uncrowded, yet within easy reach of Sydney, the aptly named Honeymoon Bay at Jervis Bay is one of a seemingly unlimited number of priceless assets which entice citizens and visitors to the coast.*

Opposite, top: *The coast south of Sydney also features rocky headlands and long stretches of sand, providing spectacular views and a variety of interesting rock types and formations. Near Bermagui, the rock glows in the clear, early morning light.*

Opposite, bottom: *Between the golden beaches, Sydney's coastline is made up of sheer sandstone cliffs, such as these at The Gap at Watsons Bay, just south of The Heads. The rock platforms at the base of the cliffs are much favoured by rock fishermen.*

Above: *South of Sydney lie hundreds of miles of accessible, unspoilt and uncrowded beaches. Jervis Bay, a short day trip from the city, is noted for its crystal waters and sparkling white sands.*

Opposite, bottom: *Clear, sheltered waters, teeming with sea life, attract sportsmen and sportswomen to diving and snorkelling. The underwater scenery and natural life can be viewed and enjoyed in safety.*

Above, right: *Behind the beaches lies the bush, home to Australia's unique fauna. Here, kangaroos play at Green Patch behind Jervis Bay.*

Right: *A beach of one's own: exploring the remote coastline of Merimbula, south of Sydney.*

Above: *The lovable koala bear, a marsupial native to Australia, is found in established colonies throughout the Sydney area and in special nature parks.*

Published by National Book Distributors and Publishers Pty Ltd
Unit 3/2 Aquatic Drive, Frenchs Forest, New South Wales, 2086, Australia

First edition 1994
Text © Laurie Ryan

Design concept Neville Poulter
Design and DTP Lyndall Hamilton
Cartography Globetrotter Travel Map
Editor Jenny Barrett

Reproduction by Hirt & Carter (Pty) Ltd, Cape Town
Printed and bound by Kyodo Printing Co (Pte) Ltd, Singapore

**National Library of Australia
Cataloguing-in-Publication data**
Ryan, Laurie
Beautiful Sydney
ISBN 1 86436 006 2

Photographs © individual photographers and/or their agents as follows:

G Adsett/APL p 16 (top left); **ATC** p 22 (bottom), p 25 (top); **Australian Picture Library** p 11 (bottom), p 30 (top); **JP & ES Baker/APL** p 24 (top); **Ross Barnett** p 7 (top), p 12, p 15 (top and bottom right), p 19 (top and bottom right), p 21 (bottom right), p 24 (bottom left), p 27 (bottom right), p 32 (top left), p 38, p 40, p 42 (bottom), pp 44-45; **Ross Barnett/APL** p 10; **Hans and Judy Beste** p 41 (bottom right); **John Carnemolla/APL** p 16 (bottom left), p 17, p 21 (top), p 23 (top), p 29 (top); **Jean-Paul Ferrero/Auscape International** p 14; **Denise Greig** p 43 (bottom right); **Gary Lewis/APL** p 11 (top); **Jonathan Marks/APL** front cover (right inset), p 20 (top), p 34 (top); **Nick Rains** front cover (left inset), back cover, title page, p 5 (top and bottom right), p 6 (bottom), p 13 (right), p 18, p 20 (bottom), p 22 (top left), p 23 (bottom), p 25 (bottom right), p 26 (bottom), p 28 (left), p 29 (bottom), p 30 (bottom), p 31 (top and bottom right), p 32 (bottom left), p 33, p 34 (bottom left), p 35 (bottom right), pp 36-37, p 41 (top right), p 42 (top left), p 43 (top), pp 46-47; **Nick Rains/APL** p 4, p 6 (top), p 7 (bottom), pp 8-9; **LF Schick/NPI** p 39 (top); **LF & OG Schick/NPI** p 48; **Paul Steel** pp 2-3; **Struik Image Library** front cover (main picture); **Taronga Park Zoo** p 26 (top), p 27 (top); **G Weber/NPI** p 39 (bottom).